Touch

Aiswarya B Pillai

WRITERS' READERS

Published by Booksthakam, India
info@booksthakam.com
www.booksthakam.com

Touch

A Booksthakam Book/ published by arrangement with the author

ISBN: 978-93-94378-69-8

Typeset and Cover Design by Cogitabund LLP
Printed and bounded in India by Manipal Technologies Limited

FSC www.fsc.org MIX Paper | Supporting responsible forestry FSC® C043100

Contents

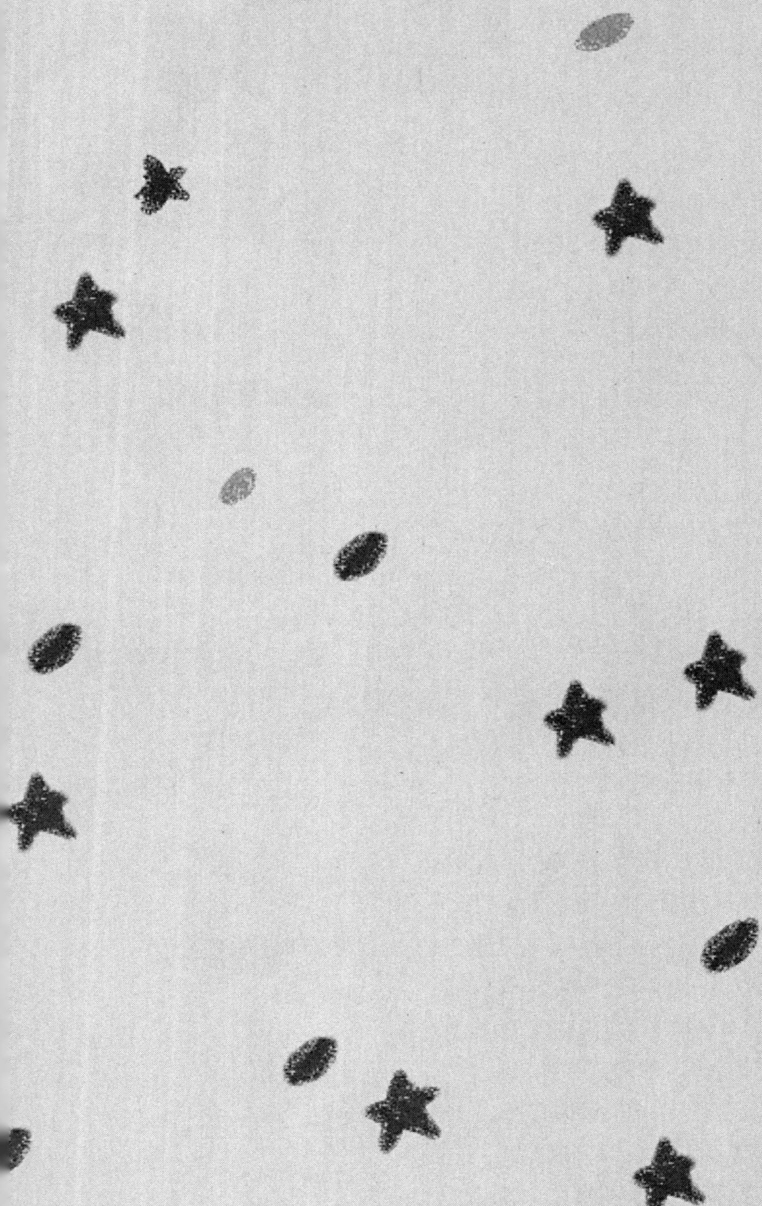

ACKNOWLEDGEMENT

A heartfelt thank you to my family for their endless love and support. You've always been there, no matter what.

To my friends - Indu and Anusree, thank you for your encouragement, laughter, and unwavering belief in me.

A special thanks to Sreelekshmi for your constant support and for always having my back.

And finally, a big thank you to myself for finishing this book. It was on my bucket list to do before I turned 30, and somehow, here we are. Sometimes, the hardest part is just starting. We made it!

FOR MY LOVE

You were the one i truly loved,
the one who made me feel beloved.

Not any soul could fathom the depths of my broken heart,
mend it all with care and attention.

If only I could be yours forever,
see you all day long and long.

If only I could live a day more,
I would like to see you all day long.

Though in utmost pain, I think of you,
the days we spend, the fun we had,
your tender touch upon my forehead,
your smile which I shall not forget.

If I could be the star that shined,
I could be with you always.

If only I knew which star you were,
I'd choose to be near you, my dear!

Death is an enemy I shall not forgive,
for you took away my reason to live!

SEASONAL FRIENDS

Friends of different shades, different views,
yet the one we love the most.

The one who brings a smile onto my face,
through your many witty ways.

All I did was trust you,
consider you as my only friend,
little did I know your truth,
hidden behind your friendly face.

You left me for your own benefits,
I did not say a word.
Then you came back to me,
when you were in need of help.

As days went by,
when trees began to shed their leaves,
All I did was shed our memories.

All your fake promises, your fake concerns,
vanished into thin air,
for all you did was hurt me.
You proved me wrong,
just like the others,
Yet another seasonal friend!

Now that I know who you truly are,
accepted the fact you're none to me,
don't come to me shamelessly,
asking for help when in need,
because i know you're only a stranger,
yes but one among my seasonal friends!

WOMEN IN CHAINS

Bound in chains, struggling for life,
every day you long to die
for the crime you hadn't done,
the sin of being born a girl.

You worship us, you respect us,
yet you tear us apart,
the tears rolling down our cheeks,
are nothing but our suppressed pain.

We neither crave for attention,
nor any caring touch,
all I need is freedom,
to live and die a women,
just devoid of fear.

Breaking the chains,
I run away, as far as I could,
where no one can hurt me.
Death is my only friend,
whom I shall trust,
it's the only gentleman who i shall befriend,
for it may hurt me only but once.

EUPHORIA

Gentle hugs and tenderness,
bringing smiles so effortless.
Hugs and kisses and rose bouquets,
and promises to be there always.
His fingers fondle through my hair,
there's nothing more for which I'd care.
The way he makes me feel,
I could not conceal.
The way he talks,
during our long walks.
The way his eyes search for me in the crowds,
my happiness just knew no bounds!

HOPE

What is hope ? I begin to wonder,
is it the vested interests of mine.
For all day long I hope to be,
a hope deep rooted in me.
Is it the thoughts I crave for,
or the expectations within me ?
I fail to recognize your so many forms,
I fail to hope for anything!

Hope isn't a word but an emotion,
an aggregate of many expectations,
whether be it the love I hope for
or the soothing wind's breeze.
I've no faith in hope nor in destiny,
for both have seemed to hurt me a lot.
Yet I hope to see you, for you are my beloved!
I wish to hold on to you as long as I could,
but fate is our enemy.
We have to part our ways,
I still hope to stay together!
Though the wind blowing reminds me of you,
I still hold my courage,
for I know and can only hope to be with you day long!

I can no longer hope for the best,
for all I had was turned to dust,
my happiness turned to deep sorrow,
my smile is fading away.
Though I may be losing,
I still, will and always do,
I will hope to live longer,
to live another day full.
Death is but a constant of life,
hoping to meet one day,
just as a long lost friend,
I hope to meet you soon!

EMBRACE THE PAIN

The lonely nights shrouded her pain,
In her pain she found her company,
all she could do was cry for help,
But the echoes of it soon faded away,
Her fears and sorrows were before her eyes,
Her existence a question before her,
Was it really worth it?
Is it worth the fight?
Her weak body could no longer bear the burden,
the burden of fulfilling expectations,
no one could see what she went through,
perhaps everyone turned a blind eye,
for it is true that sad people are just the same,
The same sorrow, the same tears,
the same broken parts,
the same shattered hopes masked by a fake smile,
the truth hurts more than the fake words,
at least the fake words are considerate,
for in the dark she realised,
the only truth worth knowing,
people change and so do you,
life changes and so do you,

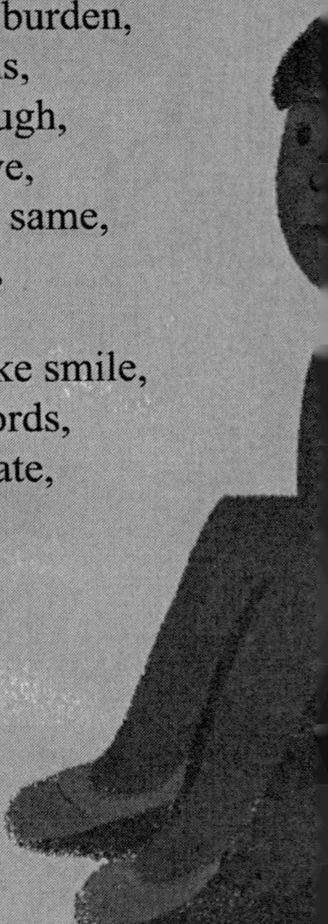

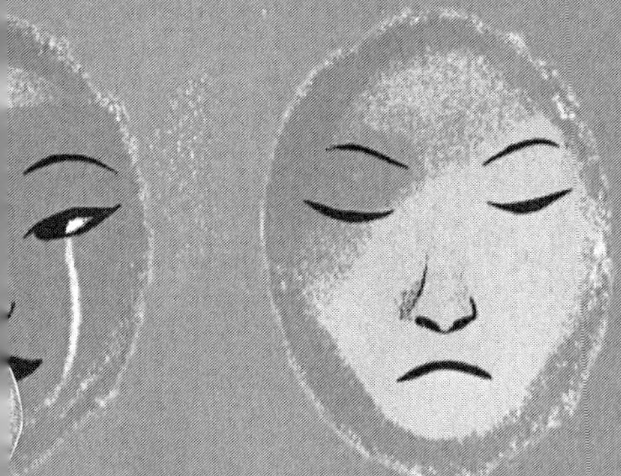

the only thing that fails to change,
is the pain in your heart,
the pain which has always been there,
through your bad times,
through your good times,
like a friend that shall never abandon,
giving you hope for a painless tomorrow,
only to face the cold hard truth,
till you realise,
it's the only friend,
the only thing that shan't leave your side,
for she was strong and determined,
she embraced the pain as her friend,
hoping it would leave her as usual,
but this time she was wrong,
though her body ached in pain,
though she couldn't bear it all,
she donned a smile, a facade,
towards the world just so fake,
for she's not lonely, she has a friend,
one that shall never leave your side,
and yes she knew for sure now,
Life's definitely worth the fight!

FREE BIRD

Born as a bird, free I may have been,
Flying over rice fields ever so green.
Feeling the warmth of gentle breeze,
Not a moment shall I spare to seize.
Fluttering my tiny yet weary wings,
Not sure what the next moment brings.
I hover over brooks and springs,
Unafraid of the petty things.
Flying away from the thorny cages,
Embracing the newfound blissful changes.
As I pass by the many strangers,
All aware of life's upcoming dangers.
Aiming for the setting sun,
A new day in my life has just begun.
All the war's lost and won,
All the mistakes that can't be undone,
Forgotten by pretty much everyone.
I know I'm not the only one,
Waiting to be a free bird in the long run!

BUTTERFLY

Fluttering my tiny wings,
passing over narrow springs,
in the gentle hands of winds,
not afraid of any things,
swiftly through the nooks and crannies,
over many mountains and valleys,
floating through the gentle breeze,
resting on flowering trees,
I finally reach the end of day,
hoping if I could just stay,
tempted towards the burning flame,
in the end what a shame,
with blazing wings of fire,
death came to admire!

LIFE; A BITTER TRUTH

Through the darkness of my life,
I wander all the way.
Is there a light, a ray of hope,
For me to cling on to it.
I wonder why I am alive,
The reason why I breathe.
If only I had a meaning to it,
I could just survive.
All the shadows that I see,
All the sorrows right before me,
All the happiness that I can’t bear,
Will it be even in my fate?
For all I know is life goes on,
With its devilish behaviour,
Causing pain to anyone,
Who questions its decisions.

If this is life,
Then what is death?
Is it just a better friend?
Now I know what life is,
A mixture of sorrow and happiness,
But sorrows in great proportion,
Wrapped in pretty ribbons red,
Hurting everyone that touches,
Burning their heart,
Draining their happiness,
Making you hope all day long,
For a better day,
For a happy moment,
That which sadly isn't in your fate!

UNREQUITED LOVE

The one and only strong desire,
Only if fate could just conspire.
Tender embrace, your gentle strokes,
All leading to painful chokes.
How I longed to stay with you,
I had the least of any clue,
Waiting desperately for a rendezvous,
Trying to figure out your point of view,
All this seems like deja vu,
With all its painful residues,
All I can say is just adieu!

VEILED DREAMS, SILENT SCREAMS

Her burning desire,
Like golden embers of fire,
The darkness in her heart,
And the secrets it imparts,
Masked her shattered dreams,
For all that remained was her screams!

FIRST FOR YOU

Wish I could be the first drop of rain,
The first wisp of grass,
The first beam of sun,
I can't be any of those,
For I chose to be the first for you.

NIGHTMARE DRESSED LIKE DAY DREAM

She embraced the darkness,
for it could mask her emptiness,
Her shattered dreams, her broken heart,
All the sorrows that it imparts,
Donning a smile,
she would beguile,
hiding her true self from everyone,
cause If they knew what would be the fun!

FALLEN LEAF

Like a stranded feather,
I wandered hither and thither.
Flowing across sun-kissed plains,
With shiny droplets from yesterday's rains.
Detached from my abode,
Stranded somewhere abroad,
A toy in the playful hands of wind,
Without any clue nor a hint!
Pass the valleys of swaying greens,
Through the forts of many kings and queens.
Up and down untrodden paths,
Hovering over playgrounds full of laughs.
Like a hippie no strings attached,
Free from every bond just detached.
Yet to reach the final spot
To be one with the soil and rot!

DESPAIR

Why does it feel so empty?
Why does my heart ache?
Will this pain fade away or will it just stay?
I long for the days when I was happy, calm and composed,
a distant self I lost ,
Would I meet again?
Is life just like this ; full of despair,
if indeed it really is then what a great shame!
The sun sets, the wind blows and life goes on,
Another day, another tale, is it good or bad though,
Only time will tell how it would be,
But one thing I know for sure,
Whatever it may be, it will be with despair.
Here I sit watching the tides,
the salty wind through my hair and
a restless heart much louder than the crashing waves.

THE EMERALD ARCHWAY

Passing through the silent streets,
filled with echoes of many heartbeats;
Silent stares and friendly gaze,
unaware of the hidden betrays.

Searching for a familiar face,
sad her heart will still yearn and chase,
then she sees the green door,
she can't help but explore.

In she goes and out she comes,
with a whistle on her lips and a tune that hums.

WINDSWEPT REVERIE

Dusty winds and cloudy skies,
Sunkissed plains just so nice,
Twists and twirls up winding roads,
Here and there it unloads,
Sitting by the open window,
Brimming with the gentle airflow,
I wonder what life has to give,
If only I could just re-live!

ELUSIVE SHADOWS: DANCING WITH DEATH

Even death seems to evade me,
so invisible that even death feigns my presence.
I long for death every waking moment,
every breath, hoping I won't take the next.
Still, it surprises me like a long-lost lover,
testing and pushing me beyond my limits.
Making me beg for its arrival to be sooner,
I wish for its cold breath,
I wish for its merciless embrace.
I hope that one day we can be together,
never to be apart,
embraced in rigor mortis,
crumbling, decaying, becoming one with the soil.
Will it come sooner? I can't wait.
I count my seconds to draw closer to death.

THE RHINESTONE'S RUSE

Mistook a rhinestone for a diamond's gleam,
Unwary of how it would shatter her dream,
Unaware of the deception,
She thought this would be an exception,
Little did she know it was a mistake,
A slithering serpent, like a venomous snake,
It coiled around her slender neck,
With a final, deadly, vicious peck,
When she woke, she realised,
For all she did was compromised,
A rhinestone in the guise of a diamond,
But deadly as the sting of a scorpion.

HEALING THROUGH LOVE

I kept on holding your hand,
afraid to let go,
little did I know you were the wrong person,
though it hurts, it made me strong,
all the words just so fake,
all the smiles just so transient,
when I fell hard,
I hoped you'd be there,
little did I know you would disappear,
but now I'm happy,
cause I found the one,
he transformed my tears to happiness,
he made me laugh with all my heart,
he's the magic shop that comforted me,

No he shan't give fake promises,
Always made sure I smile,
Made me realise the only truth,
Just love yourself,
Only then shall you he happy,
Only then shall you find love,
Nudge away all your sorrows.

VANILLA WOES

Struck as though by lightning,
You crept into my unwary heart.
You made me feel emotions unknown to me,
Made me crave your touch ,
Your smell, and lingering fingertips.
Every moment, every second, I longed for more,
And then you vanished into thin air,
Like a ghost that disappears into unknown depths,
I waited and longed for your kind words,
Despair and woe filled my heart.
Just another vanilla man, nothing special,
Just another person who hurt me the same.
Wicked was your smile , the one that I mistook,
Hollow was your heart, as empty as your promises.
Poison was your words that bled and tainted my heart,
Unbeknownst to me, you took away my sanity,
And everything that I held so dear.
I was left dry and empty,
Like the nightingale that broke its heart,
For a trivial thorny rose,
You cast me away down the gutters,
Shattered and uncertain of my very own volition.

BENEATH THE MOONLIT SKY

Under the weeping willows so solemn,
Amidst the moonlit, star-studded night,
Clad in moonshine and ethereal glory,
She walked among us mortal souls,
Scared and mesmerised by worldly possessions,
Longing for the touch of a kindred soul.

The air was filled with such a sweet scent,
That neither heaven nor earth could comprehend.
She gently walked through the moss and foliage,
Her nimble feet glowed as if like a moonstone,
Her dewy lips and crimson cascade gently flowed in the night's breeze.

All the creatures were amazed by her grace,
Never had they seen such a pure soul.
She dilly-dallied through the gentle brooks,
Laid down upon the dewy carpet,
Fixed her eyes upon the moon,
Wishing for something serene.

Startled by an unseen shadow,
Derailed from her usual musings,
She saw a figure in the mist,
Gently approached with all the caution,
A silhouette of illuminating glow,
A kindred soul, a fellow spirit,
Her happiness knew no bounds.

Holding hands and gentle embraces,
Under the moonlit grassy knoll,
He whispered in her ears words of love,
She shied away in a playful gesture,
Everything seemed to be so still,
The time itself was frozen,
Kneeling down to pick a wildflower,
She turned around to meet his eyes,
Startled and bewildered he was nowhere,
She wandered hither and thither but to no avail,
All that's left was a sparkling moonstone,
A gift from the one she truly cared,
She cherished and clasped it tightly in her fist,
Her eyes brimming with tears,
No stolen kisses, not even a farewell embrace,
Vanished like a whisper, as if never there.
Unable to bear the inarticulate sorrow,
She threw the moonstone into the abyss,
Shattered into a million pieces,
Yet not as much as her broken heart,
Drifting with a gentle gait,
She sat upon the edge of the abyss,
Gazing upon the moon and the shattered remnants that prevailed.

A LOVE LETTER TO YOURSELF

I have known you since the day you were born,
Since the day you could articulate,
The day you could express your sadness,
Your happiness, and every emotion.
I have been with you through every fall,
Every heartbreak, every pain.
I have comforted you more than ever,
And it feels like more than forever.
Now the time has come,
When you're no longer sad.
You need no gentle touch,
No warm embraces,
Or reassurances of good ahead.

You've finally attained what you desired.
My happiness knows no bounds,
For together we are happy,
And shall stay so evermore.
I see happy thoughts and cheerful moments
In the distant future ahead—
Loving ones who care for you,
And the willingness to be loved in return.
May this happiness be a constant in life,
So I may never see you cry,
So I may never see you drained and distraught.
May you never lose your kindness,
Nor become so numb and callous,
Become something you dread.
For in the end, I'll always choose happiness instead,
Happy thoughts, a soul well-fed.

WHISPERS OF THE UNCHOSEN

Oh, to be someone's first choice,
Wouldn't know how I would rejoice,
To be a priority,
But that is such a rarity.
Sadly, I'm not loved or chosen,
Not even among a dozen.
Always pursued and lusted,
In the end, left disgusted.
Always an option,
Approached with caution.
Always replaceable,
Interested until attainable.
Always a want and never a need,
Just like a misfit, gnarly weed,
Plucked and trampled, then tossed aside,
Every wish is just denied.
Crumbled and broken, I lay shattered,
With all my dreams and hopes battered.
Hoping to be someone's forever,
Wishful for that endeavor,
To be chosen, to be spellbinding.
Oh, what I would give to be so enchanting!